THE BOOK OF EVENINGS

FRANK PREM

Wild Arancini Press
2025

Publication Details

Title: The Book of Evenings
ISBN 978-1-925963-02-1 (pbk)
ISBN 978-1-925963-00-7 (ebk)

Published by Wild Arancini Press, 2025

All rights reserved:

No part of this publication may be reproduced, stored in a retrieval system, or transmitted in any form or by any means, electronic, mechanical, photocopying, recording or otherwise, without prior written permission from the publisher and author.

Artwork: Sidecar and Wild Arancini Press
Internal Images: Wild Arancini Press with Adobe Firefly

For Leanne
who is the inspiration

And for the three amigos, Julian, Chris and Janet

CONTENTS

THE BOOK OF EVENINGS

Introduction 1
   . . . for a book of evenings 3
   telephone and tabby 5
   the interview 8
   a day away from friday 14
   shhh crazy 19
   the long night 22
   digging water and kissing clouds 25
   special occasion 27
   watching the thread 30
   decisive uncertainty 33
   a thickening gloom 36
   lights out 38
   learning to twirl 41
   a pride in hands 44
   untitled - a 47
   the man who knew 49
   when she walked it was a saunter 52
   he would have preferred ribbons 55
   enough 57
   socks to tell no tales 59
   identification from height 62
   katy's scrubbing up 65

towards kansas	68
a whole hour	70
the idiot	72
the argument for noosa	74
carmen and cisco	76
tonight	78

Afterwords ... 79

Author Information	81
Other Published Works	83
What Readers Say	85

THE BOOK OF EVENINGS

Introduction

The Book of Evenings was Frank Prem's first (2003) free verse poetry collection, originally published using the author name Frank Faust.

The collection features stories set in the part of the day that takes place between sunset and sunrise. From *knock-off-work* o'clock in the evening to *get-up-and-go* in the morning.

The collection also includes poems that follow the drama of ripples and ructions that take place in a man's life following a chance encounter with a mysterious female stranger.

This small tragedy is told in *Tuesday Night at Emile's,* a stand-alone story included within *The Book of Evenings*.

Here is a unique collection of stories conveyed to you in a moving and contemporary poetic style, the way you always wished poetry would be written.

. . . for a book of evenings

he has sworn
he would stop this
but once more won't hurt
and this will be the last time
surely the last

~

it is cold out

quiet

there is sound
but receded to the status
of a murmur

his footfalls
occupy disproportionate space
in the stillness

there is no hurry
no direction
measured movement
is enough
in these abandoned streets
where life has retreated
from the fall of darkness

into kitchen and lounge
bedroom and bath

to cook and eat
wash and sleep
argue and love

he knows it is there
feels it radiated
from houses

shadowed
against windows

muffled
through the air

~

so many times
in the hours after shades
have been drawn
he has paced these streets

felt the stories
whisper into him
secrets unsuspected

only to him

drawing him back again
when he has told himself
he would listen no more

every evening
every house
every last footstep
its own ever-changing story

and he has listened
yes

but this is the last time

he has heard enough

telephone and tabby

she is home by five-thirty
says hello to the cat
serves him *whiskas*
from a can opened yesterday

but not too much
overweight
is not a good look
for a tabby

glances at the phone
no messages flashing
no calls while she was away
but the night is ahead
and it might ring
he might get on the line
to say

> *hello*
> *how are you*
> *do you remember me*
> *we met at the weekend*
> *at so and so's*
> *and I wondered if you*
> *might meet me*
> *some evening*
> *for dinner*

but tonight she's alone
with another lean meal
from a packet in the freezer

it seems a bother to cook
when there is only
herself and *tab*
who is already fed
and looking for a best place
to curl up where it's warm

in front of the tv is good
for them both
later she'll wash out the smalls
run an iron across
the white blouse of wednesday
with flowers embroidered
on the collar
in a pale shade of sky

time will pass by
will go quickly enough
with an occasional look
at the phone
until half-ten has set sail
the movie is done
and all of the news updated

she sings to herself
in the bathroom

long-brushing her hair
at this time of night
like a schoolgirl
in flannel-warm pyjamas
and long dressing gown

turns in a dance-step
that deposits the toothbrush
in a teddy bear mug

while she pictures him
in her mind
only this time
he's holding her

> *la*
> *la la*
> *la la*
> *la*

she glimpses again
the silence
that broods around the telephone

gathers the bed-book
turns to page
seventy-nine without dog-ears
then lies down
for ten minutes of reading

ten minutes more half-hoping
turns the light out
rolls on her side
and whispers

> *goodnight*
> *master cat*

the interview

well
when you've said *see ya* to the boys
at about four
you jump in the car and head for home
because there's always a few odds and sods
to be done

the missus will want to see you
and let you know a few things
and so on
until it starts rising six o'clock
when you get in the car again
and head for the pub

now there's some blokes
you know
who like to start early
and head for the one over the road there
on their breakfast break at work

then back again
for a liquid lunch
but I reckon
they must be bloody alcy's

nope
the evening session
is good enough for me

and really
if you're a bloke in this town
you have to be there
because all your mates will be in
and they depend on you

want to know what's going on
if you don't show

they'd never let up
some of them
if they reckoned your missus
was playing the dictator

so it's important

oh my word
that first touch of foam is good

a man works all bloody day
for that moment

tastes better than a woman

position is important
in the main bar

you can't stand over there
it's too close to the open fire
boil your beer
if you're not careful

a bit of distance is better
and a lot of the places are claimed
by regulars

greggy and darc
generally go to that corner

norm and freddy prop the bar
just beside the totaliser

johnno's back against the fishing club wall
over there
under the stuffed murray cod

big bastard that one was
bluey got him above the weir
in '79

yes
and so you usually end up
about here
with a bit of something
to lean against

good view across the bar
to see who's coming and going
in the place

and you want to have a sticky
at the bar-girls
of course

janie and marie
lovely girls they are

janie
organises the childrens hospital appeal
every year
it's a big deal around the place

marie's married to a blow-in
from out of town

they live on a little hobby farm
on the outskirts
five bare-arsed acres of scrub
and a hacienda

some blokes like to sit on a stool
but really you're better off
to stand and talk

there's something about the sound
of voices in the bar
around about happy hour
that just makes you feel at home

anyway
what else do you want to know

oh well
a lot of the blokes in this town
work shifts
with plenty of days off and holidays
and end up with time on their hands
now and then

so they'll come here and have a yap
with the other blokes
to see who's got a bit of cash work
on the go

you might as well
earn a bit of beer money
as spend your spare time going nuts
at home
with the missus and kids around you
all the time

it's a good place to do business
is the pub

something you should remember
if anyone happens to ask
is that you only ever have two beers
at the pub
never more

the first one and the last one

that'd be right
wouldn't it
only ever the two pots

so
by the time you've finished that second one
that I just told you about
it's pushing seven thirty
and you've got to get going
because the missus
will have dinner done
and getting cold

so you tell the blokes
hoo roo
and get gone

we don't have much trouble with the coppers
here
but it's best to be careful
and go the back way

mind you
you never know
where the buggers will turn up
these days

sometimes you'll sit down at the table
to have dinner with herself
but
often as not
you might as well sit in the lounge
and watch that *Blue Heelers* show
on telly

she'll clean up the dishes
and as likely as not
you might drift off
for a minute
catch a little bit of shut-eye

it's a long day
you know

the movie
might be worth watching
but most nights
it's easier just to go to bed
for an early start
in the morning

will that do you

all right
cheers then

a day away from friday

run the raindrops
a race to the car
throw shoulder bag and briefcase
in the back
beside the toddler seat

sit a moment
to wipe streaming hair away
from eyes
in a small smear
of dark eyeliner

not to worry
there's a spare pair
of junior-wear overalls
to wipe down face and eyes

wish there was a towel
under the debris
of picture books and toys
but
at least the day is done

windshield wipers
are almost as good as music
when all that's wanted
is sound
to act as a guide
until arrival at childcare

hello to mothers
hello to staff

 hello hello
 hug me baby girl

 hey did you miss me

 yes it's wet and it's raining

 come on
 let's get your things
 did you play today
 yes I'm listening
 tell me

chatter and wipers
rhythm and melody
all the way to the driveway

child and carry-all
shoulder bag and briefcase
and rain
to the front door

where keys are misplaced

lay down the load
instigate a fast search
then inside
and the heater
with tv for a minute

while bathroom and thick towel
turn wet hair into dry
by the hard-rubbing magic
of friction

clothes are slipped off
spread on the drying rack
while brassiere and hose
run around to find order
beneath a jumper
slacks and slippers

talk
and talk talk talk

it's busy in the kitchen
with a chirper full of rat-tat-tat
inquiry and information exchange
operating at full flight

soup
peas and potatoes
with leftover chicken
made warm and cut fine

no forgetting tomato sauce
to make it just right

the bath is warm
and bubbles
with a duck and a doll
some blocks

and a girl
preoccupied for a moment
making a noise
like a hum
or a song
and moving something important
from there
over to here

then a grin that shows traces
of sauce
and some dinner that decided
to stay but
a washer will change that

> *close your eyes*
> *here comes the scrubber*
>
> *there*
> *you're clean again*
>
> *yay*
>
> *come into the towel now*
> *I'll wrap you up*
> *like a mouse in a mitten*
>
> *try to hold still*
> *try to stay there a moment*
> *I'll help your jammies on*
>
> *do you know what this says*
> *follow my finger with your eyes*
> *while I tell you*
> *you say it now*
> *I'm listening*
> *oh*
> *that's very good*

one more last story
then turn down the light

a cuddle
a kiss

and the blanket tucked in
before quiet steps to the doorway
and a last look

leave a light on
in the hall

back to the kitchen

clean up the dishes
set the wash going
pack up toys from the floor

consider tomorrow

what time for childcare
what time for work
what to be packed ready tonight
what the schedule holds
till pick up and home
when at last
it will be friday night

a chance to put feet up
with half of a sleep-in
to follow

but that's still
a day away

shhh crazy

well
I don't mind

crazy
oh no
I

quite like crazy
but

you

are a touch

too psychotic

don't you think
you're just a little too

changeable

too

erratic

too

dramatic

you're just a bit
more
crazy
than I

can

handle

> *shhh*

I didn't say
I don't love you
silly
I love you

fine
like morning

fine

like sunlight
stars at night
I love you all right

but

> *shhh*

you're a bit

too

much

> *stop*
> *stop*
> *stay like that*

mmm
such a crazy crazy you

and

after

this

I

am going

to

    shhh

I

am

going

to

leave

    shhh

crazy

the long night

the room is darkened but a
live
to the beeping of machines
and glow of indicator lights

green and red

noisy
and yet hushed

tubing adds
a surreal air

she is in the room
seated in a chair
by the bed

red eyed when awake
dozing
from time to time

he is in the corridor
for a moment of air
and space

seeing activity all around him
seeing nothing
thinking . . . *everything*

thinking
nothing

she arrived before him
summoned from her work

he found out
when he reached the last message
on his answering machine

the uncertainty
and trauma
have affected them both

made them distraught
when already they were on edge

this has come out of the blue
and he doesn't know
how he should deal with it
if there is anything that he can do
at all

it seems out of his hands

his mind strays
to what this might mean
in their lives

to the note he left
pinned to her pillow
this morning

whether she saw it
or if there might be a chance
to retrieve it unread

whether anything should be said about it
regardless
when everything is so changed

compared to this
he and she
are a petty concern

he wanders back into the room
where a ghost figure
has checked the tubes
made some notes
silently drifted out

from a chair
he watches the bed
absorbs the regular rhythms
of breath and beep

the repetitive patterns
of green lines

thinks how long
one night
can be

digging water and kissing clouds

he must have been cold
for it is may
and there is no heat
in the descending sun

he stood
in the shallows
water above his knees
a short-handled garden spade
in his hands

and he shovelled

displacing water
in a regular
rhythmic
movement

forward and down
scoop and raise
over the shoulder

repeat

above him
a cloud-bank
has formed into lovers
engaged in a kiss

lingering
intact

as last ethereal wisps
perform an illusion of presence
all the while
stealing away secretly
until a moment
when no kiss remains

they are gone

the sun is low
the water transformed
to cobalt

the shovel wielder too
is no longer there

his impact
as ephemeral as cloud

special occasion

there is a devil in the detail
he has struggled with all day
still on his mind
as he eases into a seat
on an m-train
his laptop in-between legs
on the floor

he can't open the evening paper
the train is too crowded
and he is tired
as though the demon
has sapped him of wit
and of mind

leaving him to rock
in a stupor
as sound rushes by
reflected from retaining walls
embankments
and spray-can graffiti
on the sides of factories

he sleeps

until something in the way
the tune changes
prompts arousal

to the car
then to home

break the drive
for a bottle of ruby red

and iris
arranged in a spray

>	hello chick
>	how you going
>
>	yeah I'm tired
>
>	these are for you
>	happy anniversary
>
>	no I just want to sit by you
>	in the lounge
>	will you let me snuggle up
>	so I can breathe you
>	at last
>
>	it's been a long day
>	and lord I'm glad to be home
>	to kiss you
>	and close my eyes
>	while I touch your hair
>
>	I'd rather not eat yet
>	just sit here beside me
>	I'm drawing all my strength back
>	through you

it is a quiet slow meal
candles and merlot

then two for the dishes
shoulder to shoulder
in small talk of the day
and the comfortable static
that runs from a finger

until
it touches a finger
and both of them smile
look into the others eyes

he places an arm
around her shoulder
as they angle their way
through the door
along the corridor
to bathroom and bed

tonight it's an early one
they'll have friends
for dinner
at the weekend

watching the thread

he is preoccupied

the image in his hand
is not the best of them

not as good as the blow-up
on the wall
beside the wardrobe door

nor the carefree glance
backward
across a shoulder
in the gold-edged frame
angled towards him
from the top
of the computer box

the best
is the shot
of body in profile
with face pointed directly
at the camera
and set
now
as background wallpaper
on the monitor

so natural
a perfect presentation
of all that is good
of all that is
why

this new image warrants
only
a lesser location

some place
where a reminder
is all that's needed
and not the detail

he casts an eye
around the room
seeking out spaces
identifying potential

extends his senses
to mentally explore
each room in the house

perhaps
as part of a collage-lining
inside a drawer
in his bedroom

when he moves his socks
he will see
like an unexpected surprise

that will do very well

it is so easy
so rewarding

these pictures

what he knows already
what he has still to learn

he will know
will get to know
everything

but
no photography tonight

just being there
feeling the connection
like fine current
through a thread of live wire
almost
seeing it sizzle
from the window
to his eyes

that will be enough
tonight

decisive uncertainty

should she go
yes of course
she has to go
but
does she want to

that's the issue

he'll be there
she's almost certain
and what to do then
if he is

it isn't that he's a bad man
no
he's actually rather nice
gentle and witty
endearingly self-conscious
fun to be with

and he's interested
he's made sure she knows
he's interested
without pushing hard
but leaving no doubt
leaving the next move
to her

what to do

does she want this . . .

she's tried before
it's always a disaster
sad endings
with hurt and heartbreak
and she is at a stage
where she could easily
live without it

who needs that shit

well of course
she does
he does
everyone needs it
but is it worth it
when there is so much to risk

peace of mind that's taken years
out the window in a second

she has to make a choice soon
or he will feel disappointment
lose interest
and move on

not the kind
to hang around
where he isn't wanted
so she needs to send a message
one way or another

perhaps tonight

she will study him again
how he comes across
what impact he has on her
who he really is

what it is about him
that makes her laugh
so readily

try to touch her own feelings
and needs
assess them and work it out

then do something
act

which outfit
will look best
to send a message
of decisive uncertainty

a thickening gloom

in late afternoon
two men are walking

a man and a boy

the man is talking
intense
the boy is silent

they stop
the boy
with his back against a paling fence
the man facing him
speaking urgently

a police car slows
pulls in to the kerb

> *please step this way sir*
> *while I speak*
> *to the young fellow*
> *for a moment*

> *yes sir*
> *I'm sure that's right*
> *but just stand here for a moment*
> *thank you*

the boy responds

> *it's all right he's my father*
> *no there's no problem*
> *it's all right*

the man

> *I'm his father*
> *it's not how it looks*
> *there's a situation at home*
> *we were just discussing home*

the policeman asks again

> *yes*
> *I'm all right*

the police car pulls away
slowly

the man and boy start to walk
in the opposite direction

the man
puts an arm around
the boy's shoulder

the boy remains rigid
unyielding

as the last of the sun
fades
leaving a thickening gloom
they turn the corner
and are gone

lights out

it's absent minded
almost unnoticed
by either of them

he has a novel
she a magazine

bedside lamps
cast a comfortable glow
over her large
and his smaller
pages

he raises his eyebrow
at a florid passage

she wears her glasses low
toward the tip of her nose

side by side
each is absorbed
with reading
and he
has been rubbing his foot
against her leg

a gesture so familiar
in this comfortable time
before sleep
they hardly notice anymore

she is first
places her magazine
on the bedside table
and moves
snuggling
towards him

almost
an under-cover approach
that positions her head
on his shoulder
an arm high on his chest

her leg across his thigh
and stretched down
until toes touch

he adjusts the positioning
of arm and book
the angle of his reading
to accommodate her
while a fingertip absently traces
the topography of her spine
to the buttock

his arm presses down
on the length of her
to add a small pressure
and better feel the sensation
of her body against his

glances down at her head
and the golden tones of skin
under lamplight
the curvature
of a half-revealed breast
re-shaped by his chest

these positioning movements
are his own signal
to finish reading
drop the book to the floor
and bring both arms together
in a hugging embrace
that lets his body encompass her
for a few moments
as she slips towards sleep

one last craning of the neck
up by her
down by him
to kiss and murmur

before the lamp
is turned
off

learning to twirl

well
I don't think I was such a bad husband
not really
no worse than the rest
that much is sure
probably the dancing
gave a clue

.

.

.

pardon
oh sorry
I was just thinking a minute

you know none of the boys
that I grew up with
could dance

it's funny
my mother and my sister
both tried their damnedest
to teach me to waltz
and fox-trot
and what-have-you

they loved
being able to dance
and my mother told me
it would be important to me
in my life

but I'd have none of that
felt there was something
embarrassing
about it

we
sort of danced
when we were courting

cramped floors where
we mostly clung
for dear life

like a pair of startled bunnies

and because being so close
felt pretty wonderful
but
after we married
not really

sometimes we'd be somewhere
with a band playing
and she'd say let's dance

not necessarily waltz
often it was the modern
all-arms-and-legs stuff
but I couldn't do it
unless I'd had a skinful

I changed you know
made a decision
sometime or other
that I'd do it
get up and dance
no matter how silly I felt

was too late though
and she wasn't interested
anymore

I think I'd broken her
of any desire

and
looking back
we were probably already buggered by then
anyway

waiting for the last rites

I think
at least I wonder sometimes
if me not dancing
had something to do with it

maybe that was enough
in a way
to make me a bad husband

.
.
.

still
it's history now
isn't it

would you care for a twirl

a pride in hands

she has been through his pockets
through his wallet
looked at the collection
of receipts

read the scribbled note
on the back
of a business card

made the call
heard the voice
remained silent

understood

~

she was proud of her hands
once

soft skin
long fingers
so suited for the piano
she'd loved to play

that he
used to listen to

now she thinks them ugly
useless
knotted joints and stiffness

ragged nails

no more piano

ha

no-one to listen anyway

~

she knows where he's been
where he is right now

she shouldn't know

shouldn't have gone
searching
through his private space

but what real choice
was there

and now she is waiting
trying to decide
act the fool
or deal with it

stay or go

how

~

she rubs her hands together
listens
to the rasping sound
they make

studies the lines
and lumps

thinks
when did they
grow so ugly

TUESDAY NIGHT AT EMILE'S

CONTENTS

TUESDAY NIGHT AT EMILE'S

prelude #1 - in preparation 1
prelude #2: spot your chances (lamb and lion) 2
tuesday night at *emile's* 4
sing and be gone 9
a trial of tuesdays 11
an un-operatic shoe 15
the way to leave them 19
a small conversation 21
from the man at 24
sometimes it's dancing - old fashioned tap 26
and yet she looked so 28
who is he (1) 30
crying air 31
a connection 34
who is he (2) 38
coming home 39
you can't take them with you 42
last escort 44

prelude #1 - in preparation

his shoes are polished
the socks elegantly patterned
riding high over the ankles
as they should be

a clean shirt of pale blue
knotted bow tie with jacket
and the comfortable brown
corduroy trousers

his hair is combed straight back
and parted

the way that he likes it

he is ready

prelude #2: spot your chances (lamb and lion)

    [snap]

    [snap]

out on the street

the mean mean pavement

you have to watch
your eyes wide open

check the bad guy

around the corner

keep a distance from the losers
with nothing for you
and then

you have to spot
your chances

    [snap]

    [snap]

everybody on the street's a hustle
some will aim for subtle
some for
muscle
use your senses
to find a target
take your time (just take
your sweet time)
work it right
don't count on second chances

keep your mind well clear
put your tush in the rear
well out the way

of trouble

don't let them sneak you
from behind

    [snap]

attack is all about defences
keep yourself armed up
and ready

steady

go go go go

slow

this one's a lamb

    [snap]

you're a lion

    [snap]

    [snap]

tuesday night at *emile's*

on a tuesday
it is *emile's*
where the choices
might be as long
as five courses of menu
but *emile* already knows

the regular table is free
a sign
he hopes
of status accorded
and no mere coincidence
of day to day
restaurant trade

a window seat at a table for two
set for one
is a chance to glance out
at the slowing movement on the street

he likes to watch
the world winding down
in the evening

after a handful of banter
behind a flutter of napkin
and the chuckled low pleasure
of wine being poured
emile is gone

and glasses for reading
emerge from a pocket

the latest new scientist
is displayed
with its interesting article on a test
someone conducted in mexico
to demonstrate that . . .

. . .

in a proof that will stand
for once and for all

he nods and approves

~

she approaches

oblique

from the side

says
would he mind
the tables are so full
and she just needs to . . .

. . .

she is seated

he
hasn't quite noticed
hasn't quite spoken
his eyes move

from her
to the *scientist*
to a quick check
of tables vacant
at the rear of the room

then
back at her

she swings a sheer-coated leg
that entered his periphery
at an angle to the table
from beneath the sharp pleat
of a dance-skirt

adorned by a red shoe
that is largely heel
and taper

the movement is back and forth
mesmerising
as she talks

some part explanation
some part an appeal
some part referring to the article
he had been reading in the scientist
and some part
lost
when she leans forward
in a low cut voice
that insinuates itself
into the air
all around him

~

emile is all tut-tut
with a plate on his arm
waved away
this is no time for eating

then summoned back
she must have food
yes of course
bring another serve
keep the first one hot

his head has begun

he throbs
a little breathless
cannot utter more than a half-word

she speaks
in a manner that amazes
as a headlight might speak
to a rabbit on the road

the meal is consumed

~

he walks home
almost a stagger
his glasses
have remained
at *emile's*

all he can think of
is the sound of gunfire
that annoyed him
in a movie last night
until he turned the television off

and the image
of a shoe

to and fro

in vivid red

next tuesday
perhaps
he will speak to *emile*
for the evening was ruined
his solitude broken
she had no right
emile should have prevented
and
what was her name
has she been there before

she needs to learn
something of decorum
and perhaps
if he sees her again
at *emile's* on a tuesday
he might take the time
to inform her

sing and be gone

sometimes you have to
sing
for your supper
when the work's not there
money's not there
and the rent

is over
due

you have to dust your talents
work your assets
slip into a slinky
sheer legs and shiny
let your body
do the intro
let your body catch him
right

between the eyes

don't give the mark a minute
better wriggle
do a fidget
keep your tassels twirling
and talk

and talk

like you've never
talked
before

just tell him anything you think of
never mind the subject
got to get your pieces
in his mind in his attention

then honey
don't you know
you're supping off the menu
got yourself
a brand new best friend
eyes all over you
but
it's better not to linger

grab
whatever you've been given
then
sister

you'd better
get you

gone

a trial of tuesdays

it has been three weeks

nothing has changed

the routine remains the same
attention to the detail of appearance
is thorough

he remains punctual

emile is delighted to see him
as always on a tuesday night

ushers him to the table

is perhaps even more solicitous
than formerly
for *emile* has taken it
rather personally
as though it was a reflection
on his own character
and that of his establishment

~

the journal is placed on the table
but the glasses emerge from their pocket
a little more slowly
the gaze through the window
to the footpath and street
to the people passing by
is prolonged and pensive
lingering

from time to time
he glances around the room
briefly noting table occupants
and sighting all of the doorways

at the conclusion
of each visual circuit
a slight frown
and pursing of the lips
before return
to the pages of new scientist

~

dinner is as always
trust *emile* to see to that
though not even *emile* can
restore the sensation of taste
that was always such a highlight
but seems now
to have mysteriously vanished

replaced by a feeling
of going through the motions
chewing
without savour

it is almost a relief
to get to coffee
and the traditional snifter
of port

tuesdays
are becoming a trial

after the first week of anticipation
that took him by surprise
the second of a dawning awareness
and now
this depressing realisation

he casts another glance
around the room
nods to himself
then makes his way to the counter
to tot up the bill
share a bland pleasantry with *emile*

    good night

good night

~

a slow walk
to home
and the self-containment
that now feels a little cramped
where it had always seemed
so comfortable

just right

he hangs the clothes
in the wardrobe
takes a glass of water
to the bedside
then slides between the sheets
into a bed that seems
vast and yet
confining

the feeling
he is certain
will pass
and these vague disturbances
will cease to trouble him

but perhaps
he should consider dining
in another establishment
venturing out
to other places

perhaps

  goodnight

an un-operatic shoe

well
this is hardly the opera

still
the seats are quite fair
even if a little too distant
from the stage
to allow ideal vision

he has been told the show
is entertaining
and not just the loud thrashing
so common now

the main act has been imported
with a reputation
for performance of depth

music and lyrics

style

not bad for popular music
although
obviously
unlikely to reach the heights

gershwin owns the genre
but one can never tell
there may be something contemporary
that appeals

and after all
he has been invited
by good friends
people whose taste in such matters
is generally impeccable

~

there is something familiar
about the support act

not so much
what she is singing
standard fare really
but something about her
has begun to nag at him

she moves well on the stage
a girlish freedom
for some numbers

moments of mature stillness
for others
where she allows her voice

to do the work
without the distraction
of a lot of jiggling around

he is almost certain
that he has seen and heard her
before
but has been led to understand
she has released no recordings
so it could not be that

frankly
she is not quite to the standard
that would compel him
to buy her work
and yet
he cannot stop looking at her
peering to get the best view

there is something

~

the main act was a disappointment
nothing special about them at all

or perhaps that isn't doing them justice
for if he is honest
there were long passages
when he simply wasn't listening
caught himself deeply preoccupied
embarrassed
when a companion whispered
about the quality of a phrase
he hadn't registered

he is thinking of that girl
the support act

trying to identify the source
of his disquiet over her

it is deeply troubling
to be unable to pinpoint the problem
he is disturbed

she was wearing something in blue
but he has an image in his head
that he can't seem to dispel
of a high-heeled red shoe

moving
to and fro

frustrating
that he can't quite place it

it will come to him

the way to leave them

on a night like this

you've got to hug your words

got to make them warm
before you let them go
because

the crowd is in
looking for a show

you're on first

you want to
let them know
that it's
worth it

that you're worth it

that what you've got
is what they want to take home
when they leave

never mind

the headline act

never mind

the coughers
the talkers
the late ones coming in
with their lack
of tact

make them

focus

listen

make them want to want you
to stay awhile
hear you give
a little more

like a short encore

to salute them

make them love you
give your heart away

if they'll listen

pay attention

then bow your way backstage
while they still
need
what you're offering

that's the way

to leave them

hungry

for some more

more of you

a small conversation

emile is concerned
monsieur does not seem himself
he has become un-precise in his timing

erratic

for two weeks
he did not attend at all
on the customary tuesday night

it is becoming difficult
to hold the window table for him
this is after all
a busy establishment
and the appearance of an empty table
in a desirable situation
is not a small thing

and that is not all

monsieur appears more
absent-minded
than has been customary

he forgets to bring his glasses
sometimes stands before his table
gazing for long moments
to all parts of the restaurant

other customers have mentioned
they wonder if he is lost
or perhaps some manner of eccentric
it is most concerning

and in attire . . .

tcha

there is evidence of *deshabille*
unthinkable
in a gentleman such as *monsieur*

it was that girl

she is the cause of this
there can be no doubt

if only *emile* had seen her
before she had so inveigled herself

and *monsieur* caught off-guard
totally incapacitated
to deal with one such as she

alas

something must be done
and yet

monsieur has been such a *patron*
from even the early days
when business was not so good
as now

a little longer certainly
he is worthy
of such a consideration

perhaps a few words with *monsieur*
an expression of solicitude
polite concern

perhaps this
would not be too much to do

oui
a small conversation

from the man at

perhaps they are right
this is no way to be carrying on

but
if she is the same girl
the one that broke into his life
and stole

what

his composure

his satisfaction in an ordered life
free of petty distraction

the sense he held
of his own adequacy

if she is the same girl
he has to know

why

it had to be more
than a random encounter

why did she choose him

for what purpose

what did it mean

~

the mirror
suggests a shave
may be in order

it has become an effort to attend
to the small things

he was doing well enough
for awhile
recovering his poise
until the concert

if it was her

he will make the effort
it may be important

~

he has backtracked
to discover the performers
name

her name

taken steps to establish
where she will next appear

tonight he will be there
will try to see her in the break
or after the performance
he has to know

a dozen roses
lie on his bed

tightly rolled ruby buds
dark at their edges

> *. . . from the man
> at emile's*

sometimes it's dancing - old fashioned tap

start your feet moving

tap-eta-tap-eta-tap

set your arms in motion
make it light
speed
and dazzle

tap-eta-tap-tapping

[CLAP]

shuffle around the issue
don't break the rhythm
backwards is a special

[CLAP]

start another pattern
ratchet up to blinding
never stop smiling

[CLAP]

shimmy like the devil
hold eye contact
keep on dancing

[CLAP]

use the light to sparkle

[CLAP]

slip behind the smokescreen

[CLap]

don't forget your roses

[clap]

keep on dancing

    tap-eta-tap-eta

    tap

and yet she looked so

a disaster

it was not her
he should have known

she had never seen him before
knew of no *emile*

> *thank you for the flowers*
> *but I have to perform another set now*
> *good luck finding your lady*

no
she owned no red shoes

he knew as soon as she spoke
it could not be this one
the voice was not right

yet she looked so

he had been certain

so familiar

he must be going mad
pursuing a phantom
and for what

his life
has become unrecognisable

a mess

his head aches
from the noise
of his thoughts

he has difficulty swallowing
through a lump that has formed
as though ready to . . .

soiled
he feels somehow soiled
and cannot resist brushing
at imagined specks
of litter on his jacket

he must go home to wash
to think
this cannot go on

she was so familiar
he could have sworn

go home

stop being a fool

who is he (1)

who is this man
I'd like to know
to seek me in places
he has no right to at all

he was a moment
just one
long distant ago

we all have to keep moving
~

flitting through darkness
to watch him home

he seems a world full of troubles
does he believe me the cause
of the tempests and storms
that he carries inside

I meant no wrong to him
sought only for myself to survive
nothing more

I never aimed for his heart

what right has he to despair
when I did nothing to him

nothing
at all

crying air

there is a dizziness

he does not believe
it comes from wine
or lack of food
though he has drunk enough

eaten little

it is a morning thing
the over-rapid spin
of another morning

he does not rise from the bed quickly

has learnt
on previous occasions
that would be an error

so he remains beneath the blanket
quite still
the same unmoving way
he sleeps though the night
blinking now
to adjust to sunlight

the purpose of movement is
in any case
a moot point
for there is nothing to do

nowhere to go

when his vision has settled
the lank frame
levers feet to floor

torso upright
on the edge of the bed
from which vantage
he can survey the wreckage
no not wreckage
disarray
of the place where he lives

what was his home

now more a repository
of clothes and objects strewn

of dishes unwashed

just as he is unwashed
and strewn

he feels an acute anguish at the sight

so much so wrong
every day a torture of emptiness
the like of which
he hasn't experienced
since

not since then

how would she feel
to see him like this
this slide into dark places
when she took
such pride in him

always

her perfect young man
who did what was good
what was right

made her so proud to see him
dressed well
conducted himself like a grown up
a gentleman
right from his first outings
as little more than a toddler

she would be horrified
never mind the reasons

appalled and shamed

his shoulders begin to shake
and he takes an audible gasping breath
that is more sob
than it is air

a connection

hello mama

his approach
has been along the gravel path
beneath trees and open sky
by turns

he has meandered
to take in the old headstones
contrast them with newer trends

a dithering indirect approach

but at last he is here

the shirt is pink and creased
but at least clean

he has found his jacket
attempted a tie
although crooked

his face is more shaven
than not

the posy of flowers
a vibrant array of bright colour
just as he remembers her to have been
when he was still small

hello mama

he is uncomfortable
not knowing if he should stand
or sit

or even perhaps kneel

settles for a stoop
that turns into a sit
after he has found a small weed
to pull

he is unaware in his awkwardness
of a cloaked figure
slowing for a moment
to watch him
before continuing on the path
to some personal destination
among the untroubled at their rest

> *it's been a long time mama*
> *and I've been lost*
> *so*
> *so lost*

his face wrinkles into creases
and tears start to fall
but now
he is untroubled by them
knows he will shed a burden

believes this with all the faith
of one who has seen his first light
and knows that at last
there is a direction

as he speaks and weeps
his hand wanders
backwards and forwards
across the granite rubble
atop the grave

letting the sound of stones
gently colliding against each other
punctuate his phrases
his admissions of weakness
and fall

speaks quietly
of his bewilderment
at the cause

a fleeting episode
that caught him so unawares
obsessed and almost drove him
to an oblivion

as the narrative progresses
the tears slow and stop

breathing comes easier

his hands are still shaking
but he knows
he has passed some crucial point

hardly realises how much time
has gone by
until a cool breeze
ruffles the back of his neck
to announce that it is already evening

    goodbye mama

he pats the headstone
uncertainly
almost expecting a return warmth
finding only cold granite

still
it is enough
to form a connection

who is he (2)

in a place of endings
does he seek rebirth

among these stone-bordered ghosts

among shadows

what hope does he seek
what heart to find

he is weeping

are the tears that are falling
spilled over me

what does he mean

this man is dangerous
makes me responsible
for the way that he feels
the state of his mind

why does he cry
what did I do

what should I do

what have I done to him

what is he doing

to me

coming home

monsieur
it is so good to see you
such a long time

apologies
emile was not able to greet *monsieur*
when he entered

for the unfamiliar table

the fare has been to the satisfaction
of *monsieur* . . .

the waiter attentive . . .

bon

monsieur will drink the coffee
with *emile*

non
non
it will be so

monsieur has been missed
emile often wonders
what has become
of him
why he no longer
is a visitor to the establishment

has *monsieur* been away?
is he quite well?
he has perhaps been ill?

tcha
it is better
to not speak of such matters

emile remembers
last time he saw *monsieur*

so very worried

and then *monsieur* is gone
into smoke
such as the foolish chef
emile has had to employ
might make

oh
if *monsieur* only knew
of *emile's* trials
the staff

he would shed
the tears of rage
together with *emile*

monsieur appears better now
though
changed

emile is a sensitive man
can comprehend when the scar
has been placed
upon the soul

but
monsieur is back
and it is wonderful

monsieur
even the *cicatrix* is
in the end
only a marker of the past
non

next week *monsieur*
the usual table

emile will ensure no other
has the privilege
to sit at the table of *monsieur*
non

monsieur
emile says welcome

after such passage of time

welcome
welcome

you can't take them with you

can't take them with you

you can't take them with you

sometimes you want to love them
all night long
sometimes you want to keep them
when they ought to be gone

sometimes

you want to keep them

but you can't take them with you

on the days when you reach them
the days when they reach you
you really want to keep them

pressed in an album
like a rose flavoured prize
the perfume to let you have them
all over again

but
you can't
take them with you

so
leave them standing in the aisle
with your voice
in their heads

filling up their senses
from the songs that you sang
in a promise they'd be with you
wherever you might go

a little lie to hold them
till the end of the show
when

you can't take them with you

you can't take them with you

no

last escort

she is walking away now
has observed him
taking his leave from the restaurant
followed him to his home

studying him
to establish a measure
in her mind
of the ways he has changed
since that first encounter

she remembers it well
his face
his voice
the deep consternation
her appearance caused

and the differences visible in him
on the evening he had confronted her

oh yes
she'd denied it innocently
and he
poor fool
believed her

such a gullible man
but a sweetheart for all that

she has watched him
from concealment
on more than one occasion
since then

this will be the last time
a kind of farewell
in the form
of an invisible escort
to his door

but she will not forget

even now
unbidden
an attar of those red blooms
already long pressed into keepsake
plays in the air
about her

a sentient reminder
of the man from *emile's*

untitled - a

I know it's crazy
but
she was the first one
that I saw
in oh so long

I almost fell right there
on the spot

wanted to ask her
to touch me
had to fight
to hold back my hands
from reaching out
to stroke her skin

I knew
what I'd feel
like
she had an aura
and
I had an aura

as though
we were meant
to come together
but I

.

.

.

I wonder what she's doing
now

if she felt the thing
that I did

I never asked her
never spoke

I never saw her again

but I think about that feeling
and wonder

I work my way
to night-time
and I wonder

the man who knew

he could tell when he touched the door

there had been no signs
no clues or expectations
but
the moment the hand that held the key
came in contact with the door
he knew

perhaps an absence of vibration
or a hollowness
seeping from around the edges
of the door-frame

perhaps nothing

who knows
how the senses intuit or infer

he stopped
with the key halfway into the lock
and wondered
if he should retrace his steps

get back into the car
return to work for an hour
then start out for home again

but that
wouldn't change anything

he knew

~

when a voice speaks into silence
it can jar

sound over-loud

but in a moment
the emptiness will assert itself
and reply
with a touch on the shoulder

a shiver
along the spine

footsteps echo
like a cathedral funeral
reverent and ominous
while familiar objects
become mysterious messengers
mutely trying to communicate
matters of great moment

if only

great matters of
if only

and the scan of these
once-familiars
leads inevitably to the new item

the one supported
by cut-glass
salt and pepper shakers
gifted on the big day
so long ago

a stark white rectangle
with his name

addressed in the tell-tale loops
that once suggested open fields
and laughter

it beckons

~

the quiet can be a companion
when any noise
would be an intrusion
in the hours past darkness
spent thinking
and wondering

so many possibilities to consider
so many ruled
improbable
by the fact of the envelope

thinking the worst
dismissing the benign
reviewing all that he knows
and can recall

deep in an armchair
in the dark
the only sound
rhythmic tapping
of an unopened communication
against a twitching leg

he cannot
work it out in his mind
but he knows

he just knows

when she walked it was a saunter

she was humming in the bathroom
the kind of hum that made him think

>*she's happy*

he drew his mind back to the paper
something said about the world
about the state
about the town
something said
about the neighbourhood

she stepped across the room
and he noted when she walked
it was a saunter
the way a model on a catwalk might

to draw attention
to the length of her legs
beneath the towel
she wore high

an armful of blanket
and the two pillows
she leant to lay out on the floor
in an arrangement

a set of *look-at-me*
languid half-steps
across the room
to press a button
that filled the air with music

then
a sashay
that threw away his paper
grasped his hand
brought him to his feet
so she could dance

he watched the dreaminess
in her eyes
as she swayed
drops of water
still beaded on her shoulders
from the shower

felt heat
rising from her body
drew her close to fit him
turned her around
on their dance-floor
and as the music hit crescendo
they stopped

.
.
.

she wore the special taste
on her lips
folded further into his arms
and with the surrender of the towel
he fell in love

all over again

~

it seemed just a moment
but the sun had gone
afternoon
had wandered into evening

while they lay with each other
another day
had disappeared

into night

he would have preferred ribbons

but opportunities for ribbons
were few

he thought about
other kinds of clasp
holders of one kind
and another

but they wouldn't do

didn't convey

in the end
it was rubber bands
thick red ones
slim and stretchy brown
sad yellow

the rubber bands
holding his letters
in neat arrangement
collected in their ones and twos
each evening
when he checked the mail

even if it was only
a few bills
or a couple of pamphlets
a rubber band brought the news
held the words

he rolled them away
from the envelopes
placed them in a kitchen drawer

one band on top of another
one pile
beside the next

opened the drawer
every night
from monday through friday
steadily
not to disturb
added the newest band
to the latest pile

one day
when she comes
she will see them
and understand

make it
unnecessary
to collect them
anymore

enough

she was at the bar with a friend
when he bowled up to say hello
larger than life after all these years

full of bounce

told all that had happened to him
marriages divorces children
work
play

all in the space of a breath
how wonderful it was to see her
she looked good
have to run
see you again soon maybe

all in the space
of a breath
that left her without air

so many years

he had left the town young
heard of
every blue moon or so

glimpsed in the street
sometimes
on a family visit

as children they had played
gone to school
kissed on a new year's eve
once

might have grown close
but
probably wouldn't have

and then he was gone
into memory
and the wide blue yonder

she had stayed local
worked local
married local
divorced local

under the local eye

a life lived small and contained
but enough
mostly

it's only on days like these
up early to open the shop
to sort papers and stock
before the first customers

days like these
with his pleasure at seeing her
and his humour
his stories
still bouncing inside her head
she wonders
if it really is enough

if it ever was

socks to tell no tales

it is a sock

a grey school-sock
from one of the boys

on the mat
outside the front door

curious

herd the boys in
set the packages down
start the kettle
a cup of tea and then

.

.

.

the window is open
not much
but open

it wasn't left like that

slowly
to the bedroom

knick-knacks
from the bedside cupboard
huddled on the floor

another sock

drawers open
the bed oddly angled

some things look different
some the same
surreal

the lounge room

empty compact disc holder

the spare bedroom

no lap-top
game-boy and dvd's gone
a backpack
unable to be accounted

mess on the floor

nothing broken
just mess
a vague awareness
of absence

prickling

send the boys to the neighbours

    I SAID NOW

check all the rooms
under beds
in cupboards
never mind what's gone
make sure no-one is there

call the police
no tidying
till they get there

only a few hours

wait
learn that socks
eliminate fingerprints
that the backpack
carries the take

this happens
all the time
there is no danger
don't forget to do the insurance
in the morning

put it out of your mind
go to bed

rest easy

identification from height

> *ahum*

> *ahum*

> *shelter me from storms*

> *ahum*

there's a monotony that comes
from living in the tree-lined
the leafy streets that promenade
all up and down the smallness
of this tiny town

a figure is at the bed
in a room in a house
leaning across to bathe the brow
of a restless soul
tossing and turning
running into fever
in the drenching of a torrid time

singing little snippets

underneath her breath
like a crooning angel
ministering by mouth
at a pace that surely surely
must bring deliverance

> *baby*
> *baby*
> *baby*

she sings

baby you'll be fine

your mama's
on the job

mama takes no prisoners
baby she'll stop dragons
from sneaking in
to take advantage
mama's by your side

baby baby babe

maybe that isn't what she said
she might have sung some song
about the sinking of a boat
in the middle of a flood
while she was bathing off the sweat

I only know the wind blew
and shook a leafy branch
or two
up against a window
of a house that hugged the street
in a small town
dressed in brick and wood disguises

that every place and every one
every tree that stood the kerb-sides
was like a replica

and rising above them
in heated levitation
through a fog that yielded
reluctantly

to clarity of sight
and identification of the patterns
of the houses
the allotments
of the avenues
the straight and the winding roads

that there was *nothing*
to choose between them

they are all the same
when you see them from the sky
when you kiss them all
and wave
stretching out your hand . . . your fingers

for goodbye

except for one place where a woman
reaching with a washer
croons in a low voice
singing you back
to where you are the one
truly the only one

> *baby baby*
> *I'm calling you a way*
> *whispering the path*
>
> *baby come on home*

home

katy's scrubbing up

mama's checking out the make-up
rummaging
for things she hasn't seen since
well
let's say
they've been missing awhile
but
she thinks she might know
where to find them

they'll be in katy's room

katy's scrubbing up tonight
glitter in her hair
she's had the beauty parlour treatment
to look gorgeous
for the ball

    cha cha cha

for dancing

fourteen years and six feet tall
slender as a model on the cat-walk

she'll be black off the shoulder
pink in a shawl
a little colour on the cheeks
dark eye-liner
and yes
that'll be the missing mascara

and the lipstick

those two
will be gone awhile

it's time for girl business
in the bedroom
but papa
have you charged the camera

because here she comes now
look at her would you
just look

we always knew
but
just look at her

strike a pose by the mantle shelf
underneath the painting
we brought away from grandma's house

she might not approve of black
but she'd be just so proud of you
and happy

little brother please
remove yourself
this is not your picture
or your time

you'll have to wait your turn

papa take katy now
it's time she made her entrance

no
you won't need to carry
the shotgun

she'll be fine you know
she's a big girl
still your baby
but she'll be fine

he'll be worried all night
fretting like a

well

like the father whose baby
is taking steps into the world
and away

nervous

keep him busy if you can
talk motor cars

help him do something
with the radiator
or the carburettor
until one o'clock
or so

until she gets home

towards kansas

he has listened to the story
of a wonderful life
a tragic affair
high
low
swinging
exhilaration
despair

watched her eyes
welling tears that brimmed
but never broke
as she herself has not been broken

though close
so very close

dorothy in a whirlwind
turning and contorting still
searching desperately for a way
to click heels together
while riding and feeling
every whipping lick
the twisted beast can lash at her

let there be a landing
but don't make it too fast
just make it be there

in reach
when the moment comes

as she spoke
he could hear the elemental roar

feel it
touched by chill tremors
while swept along
in a small part of the journey
with her

and now it is done
she has told the tale
and gone
to face the next storm
already bellowing its presence
in her mind

the house is quiet again
the world outside
the same as it was

the same as it always is

night has fallen
and he
so restless

unfulfilled

a whole hour

whoa
settle down honey
we haven't even started yet

you don't want to fly
before we leave the ground
now do you
hmmm

why don't you just
hop in to the shower for me
like a love
while I fix some pillows
and a towel
my special oils
and essential equipment

or is that
the other way around

you'll love some of these

are you watching me
from in there
take a look at this

nice huh

so
come on out
dry yourself off

lie down on your back a moment
while I take a little look at you

uhuh

I'll just slip this
on
for you

hmmm
you like that don't you
I can tell

now

what would you like to do
to get us started

what would you like
hon

no rush
we've got
a whole hour

the idiot

he's as loud as a damned circus
the idiot

this is getting beyond a joke

he's obviously stinking drunk
singing and shouting
by turns

such an idiot

she has been tolerant
but it's enough

the neighbours

god knows
what they think already
and now this carousing
as though he could possibly think
it would do him any good

he can't even sing
when he's sober
and this is just awful

look at him
a bottle in his hand
a fence to lean against
and a bloody stupid song to sing
at the top
of his bloody stupid voice

calling her name now

he's fallen over
that's *IT*

> *LISTEN TO ME YOU FOOL*
> *GO AWAY RIGHT NOW*
> *OR I'M CALLING THE POLICE*
>
> *WE'RE FINISHED*
> *DO YOU HEAR ME*
>
> *GO AWAY*
>
> *I'M CALLING THEM NOW*

see what that does
surely he'll leave soon

she'll have to call them

more damned fuss

idiot

the argument for noosa

he pointed a finger

> *I think you forget*

he said

> *where you came from*
>
> *where you've been*
>
> *I think you've forgotten*
> *what you were*
> *and what made you*
>
> *I don't forget*

he spoke to her face
directly to her eyes

> *I remember*
> *every dreary day*
> *and every dirty moment*
>
> *I remember you*
>
> *I'll always remember who*
> *you were*
> *and know*
> *what you are now*
>
> *don't think you can forget*
> *just because*
> *you're in a different place*
>
> *have a care how you go*

he looked at her
another long moment
turned
and walked down the pavement
to the corner

where the traffic light turned
from

    don't walk

to

    walk

without need for him to break
his crooked stride

she watched until the white
of his back
had shrunk and faded
with the distance
and the night
shuddered once
then contemplated a long season
in noosa

carmen and cisco

she said

> you and me
> should dance latin
>
> salsa is in
> and I know I'd look good
> in flowing skirts and ruffles
>
> I can see you as a gaucho
> sharp tight pants
> and clicking boots
>
> we could hold roses
> between our teeth
> while we're stamping
> our feet
> on the floor

she said

> I want to dress
> in black and red
>
> your senorita carmen
>
> watch the way I shape my arms
> and sway my hips
>
> hold my head up
> proud
>
> come on cisco

she said

> come on

> do you think
> we could dance latin

> will you take me out stamping
> tonight

tonight

it's cloudy
but clear
cold
with a breeze

quiet

he watches clouds swirl
around the stars

wonders

is there anyone thinking of him
tonight

Afterwords

Author Information

Frank Prem has been a storytelling poet since his teenage years. He has been a psychiatric nurse through all of his professional career, which now exceeds forty years.

He has been published in magazines, online zines, and anthologies in Australia, and in a number of other countries, and has both performed and recorded his work as spoken word.

He lives with his wife in the beautiful township of Beechworth in North East Victoria, Australia.

Connect with Frank

Find Frank at his website www.FrankPrem.com, or through Social Media online at Facebook, X (Twitter), Instagram and YouTube.

Other Published Works

Free Verse Poetry

Small Town Kid (2018)
Devil In The Wind (2019)
The New Asylum (2019)
Herja, Devastation - With Cage Dunn (2019)
Walk Away Silver Heart (2020)
A Kiss for the Worthy (2020)
Rescue and Redemption (2020)
Pebbles to Poems (2020)
The Garden Black (2022)
A Specialist at The Recycled Heart (2022)
Ida: Searching for The Jazz Baby (2023)
From Volyn to Kherson (2023)
Alive Is What You Feel (2023)
White Whale (2024)
Pilgrim Volume 1 - Illustrated by Leanne Murphy (2024)
A Poetry Archive Volume 1 (2024)
A Poetry Archive Volume 2 (2024)
A Poetry Archive Volume 3 (2024)
A Poetry Archive Volume 3 (2024)

Picture Poetry/Spoken Image

Voices (In The Trash) (2020)
The Beechworth Bakery Bears (2021)
Sheep On The Somme (2021)
Waiting For Frank-Bear (2021)
A Lake Sambell Walk (2021)
A Few Places Near Home (2023)
The Cielonaut (2024)

What Readers Say

Small Town Kid

A modern-day minstrel. Highly recommended.
—A. F. (Australia)

Small Town Kid is a wonderful collection.
—S. T. (Australia)

Devil In The Wind

Trust me, this book will stay with you. Bravo!
—K. K. (USA)

Moving, beautiful, and terrible. I was left with a profound sense of respect, as well as a reminder that we should never take for granted every precious every moment of life.
—J. S. (South Africa)

The New Asylum

Words can't do justice to the emotional journey I travelled in (reading this collection).
—C. D. (Australia)

If I had to pick one book over the past year that has truly resonated with me, this would be it.
—K. B. (USA)

Walk Away Silver Heart

Instantly grips you by the throat in his step-by-step story of survival. Bravo!
—K. K. (USA)

Outstanding!
—B. T. (Australia)

A Kiss For The Worthy

A Celebration of Life Written in Thoughtful Bursts of Poetic Expression
—C. M. C. (United States)

With every verse, I found myself reflecting about myself, my life, and the world.
—K.

Rescue and Redemption

The passion of love in its many forms explored by one for another.
—J. L. (United States)

I've enjoyed every word, every breath. Every moment within the life of these stories.
—C. D. (Australia)

Sheep On The Somme

Museums and archivists take note~sell this in your gift shops, preserve it in your archives. Professors, teachers~share with your students.
—A. R. C. (United States)

(This) book is a beautiful and graphic tribute to all those brave men and women who gave their lives for their countries between 1914 and 1918.
—R. C. (South Africa)

Ida: Searching for The Jazz Baby

I found myself deeply moved by the presentation of Ida's elusive, illusionary life.
—E. G. (United States)

He gives her a depth and vulnerability that the press didn't.
— A. C. (United Kingdom

The Garden Black

Prem creates verse that illuminates our world, its experiences and history.
—S. C. (United Kingdom)

Prem's poetry reminds that life is fragile and fleeting ... both harsh and beautiful.
—D. G. K. (Canada)

A Few Places Near Home

The author has captured many beautiful images in this book, and is a wonderful photographer as well as a poet. This book would make a beautiful coffee table book filled with moving prose to make us ponder with gorgeous accompanying images.
—D. K. (Canada)

www.FrankPrem.com

www.ingramcontent.com/pod-product-compliance
Lightning Source LLC
Chambersburg PA
CBHW072109110526
44590CB00018B/3380